ANDREW LLOYD WEBBER™

THEATRE SONGS

To access companion recorded accompaniments online, visit:
www.halleonard.com/mylibrary

"Enter Code"
2330-1332-1302-6778

Andrew Lloyd Webber™ is a trademark owned by Andrew Lloyd Webber.

ISBN 978-1-5400-2438-1

HAL•LEONARD®

Visit Hal Leonard Online at
www.halleonard.com

Contact Us:
Hal Leonard
7777 West Bluemound Road
Milwaukee, WI 53213
Email: info@halleonard.com

In Europe contact:
Hal Leonard Europe Limited
Distribution Centre, Newmarket Road
Bury St Edmunds, Suffolk, IP33 3YB
Email: info@halleonardeurope.com

In Australia contact:
Hal Leonard Australia Pty. Ltd.
4 Lentara Court
Cheltenham, Victoria, 3192 Australia
Email: info@halleonard.com.au

CONTENTS

Pianists on the Full Version Recordings:

[1] Brian Dean   [2] Brendan Fox   [3] Ruben Piirainen   [4] Christopher Ruck   [5] Richard Walters

Pianists on the 16-Bar Recordings:

* Brendan Fox   ** Richard Walters

ANYTHING BUT LONELY
from *Aspects of Love*

Music by ANDREW LLOYD WEBBER
Lyrics by DON BLACK and CHARLES HART

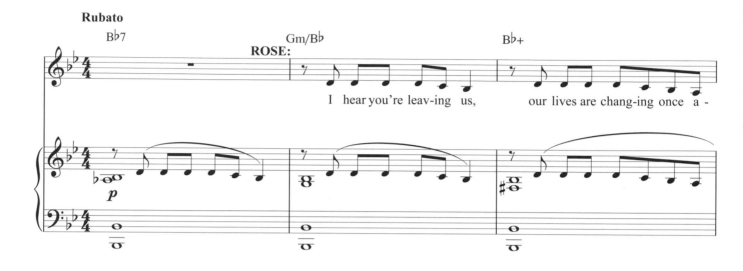

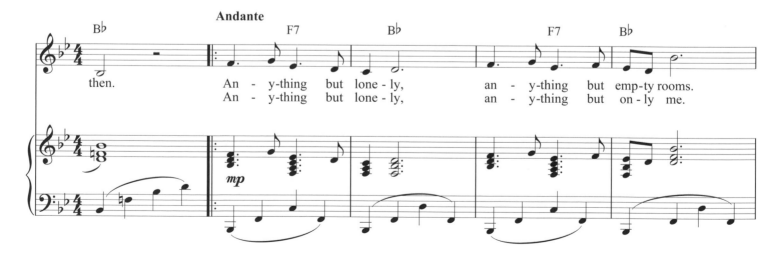

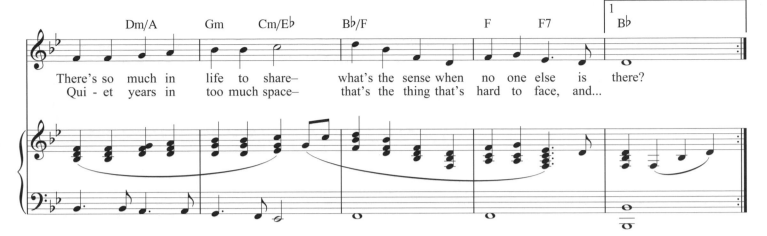

There's so much in life to share— what's the sense when no one else is there?
Qui-et years in too much space— that's the thing that's hard to face, and...

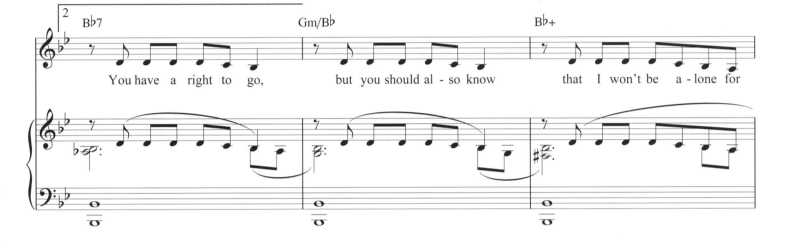

You have a right to go, but you should al-so know that I won't be a-lone for

long. Long days with noth-ing said are not what lie a-head—

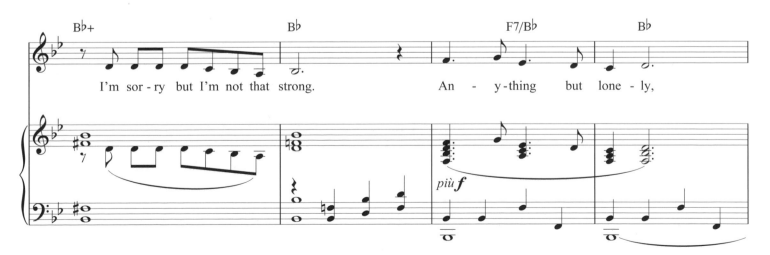

I'm sor-ry but I'm not that strong. An - y-thing but lone-ly,

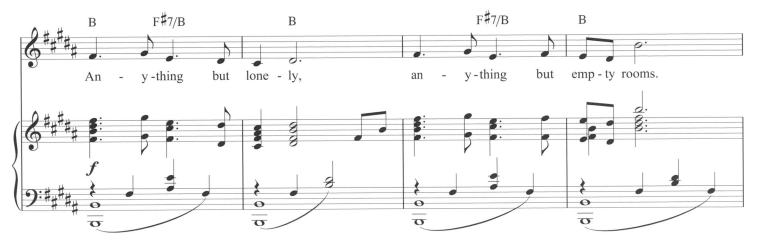

An - y-thing but lone - ly, an - y-thing but emp-ty rooms.

There's so much in life to share— what's the sense when no one else is

there? What's the sense when

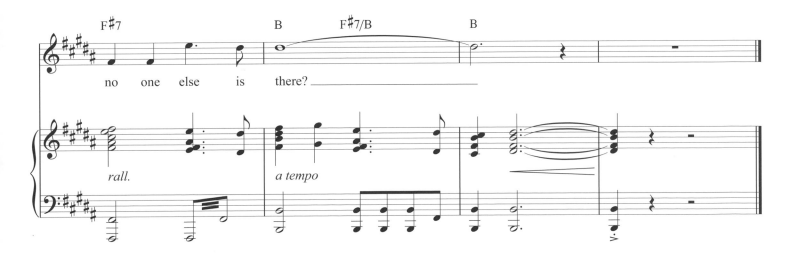

no one else is there? _____

ANYTHING BUT LONELY
from *Aspects of Love*
excerpt

Music by ANDREW LLOYD WEBBER
Lyrics by DON BLACK and CHARLES HART

DON'T CRY FOR ME ARGENTINA

from *Evita*

Words by TIM RICE
Music by ANDREW LLOYD WEBBER

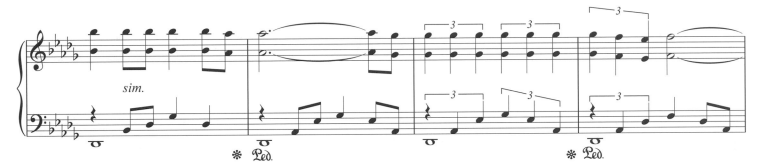

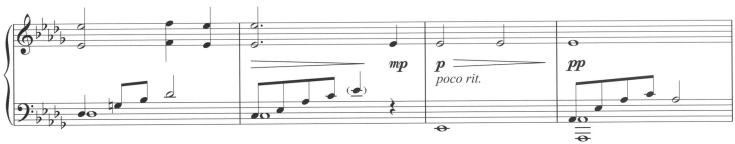

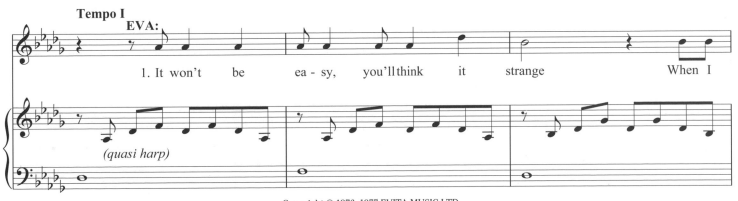

1. It won't be ea-sy, you'll think it strange When I

Slow Tango feel

for-tune and as for fame— I nev-er in-vi-ted them

in: Though it seemed to the world they were all I de-sired.

They are il-lu-sions, they're not the so-lu-tions they

prom-ised to be, the an-swer was here all the time____ I

But all you have to do is

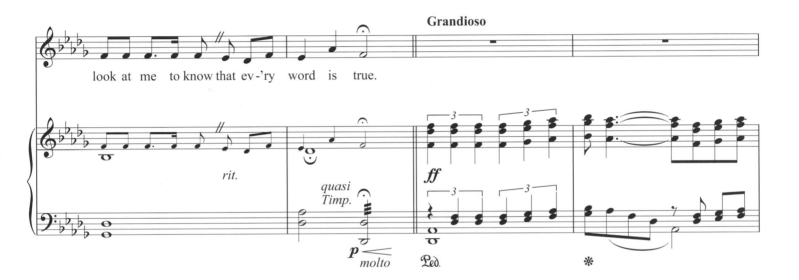

Grandioso

look at me to know that ev-'ry word is true.

rit. *quasi Timp.* *ff* *p* *molto* ℘ed. ✳

poco rit. *p* *f*

℘ed. ✳

DON'T CRY FOR ME ARGENTINA

from *Evita*

excerpt

Words by TIM RICE
Music by ANDREW LLOYD WEBBER

I DON'T KNOW HOW TO LOVE HIM
from *Jesus Christ Superstar*

Words by TIM RICE
Music by ANDREW LLOYD WEBBER

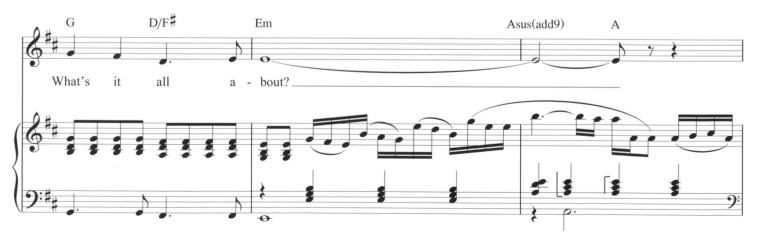

Don't you think it's rath-er fun - ny

I should be in this po-si - tion? I'm the

one who's al-ways been So calm and cool

no lov-er's fool run - ning ev - 'ry

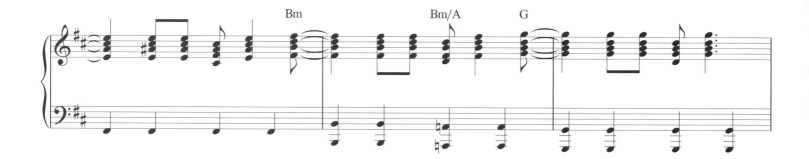

loved me, I'd be lost I'd be fright - ened. I could - n't

cope, just could-n't cope. I'd turn my head,

I'd back a - way, I would - n't want to know. He scares me

so. I want him so. I love him so.

I DON'T KNOW HOW TO LOVE HIM

from *Jesus Christ Superstar*

excerpt

Words by TIM RICE
Music by ANDREW LLOYD WEBBER

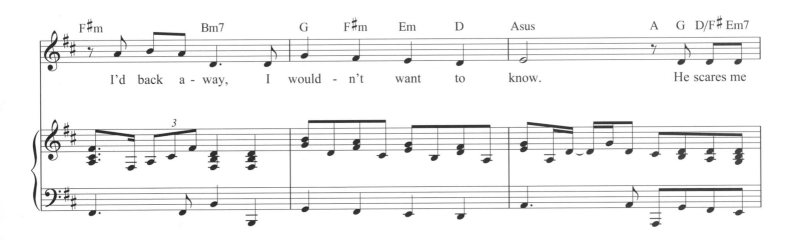

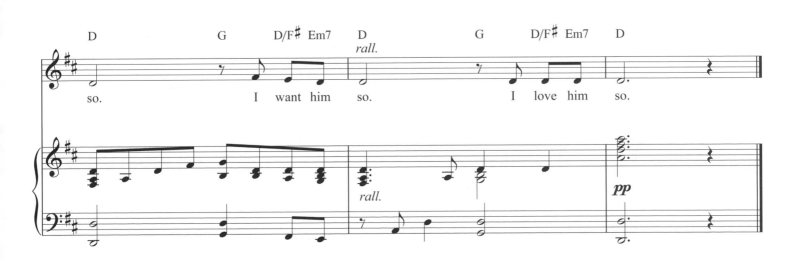

THE LAST MAN IN MY LIFE

from *Tell Me on a Sunday*

Music by ANDREW LLOYD WEBBER
Lyrics by DON BLACK

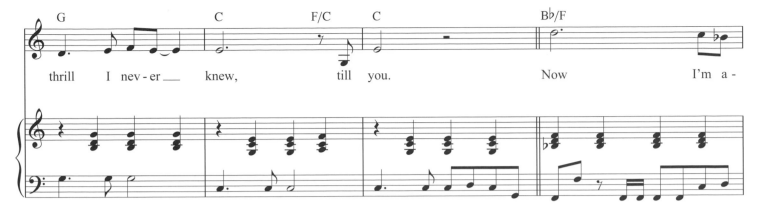

thrill I nev-er ___ knew, till you. Now I'm a-

live in-side, I'm glow-ing, I'm how I want to be, lov-ing

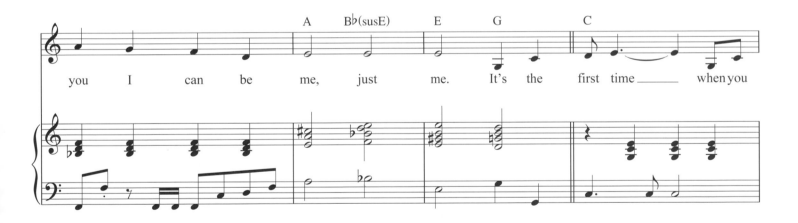

you I can be me, just me. It's the first time ___ when you

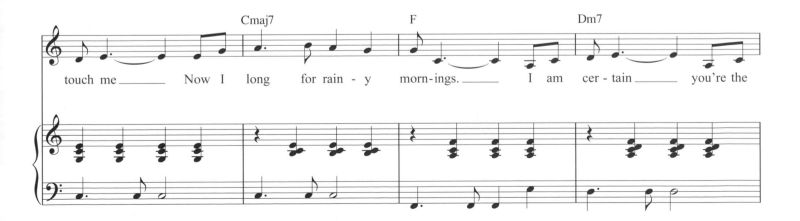

touch me ___ Now I long for rain-y morn-ings. ___ I am cer-tain ___ you're the

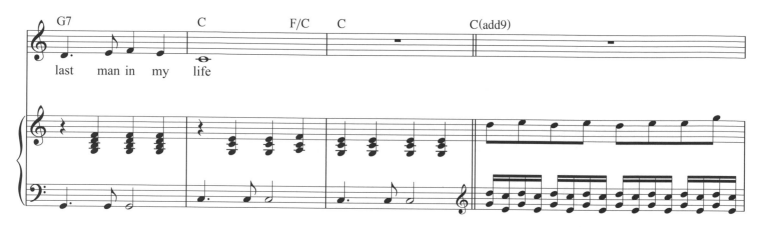

last man in my life

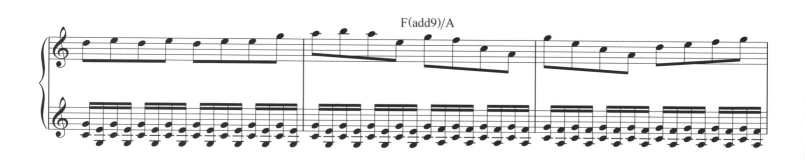

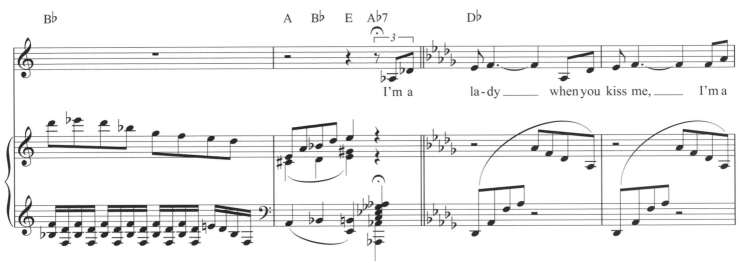

I'm a la-dy_____ when you kiss me,_____ I'm a

child when you are leav-ing._____ I'm a wom-an_____ ev'ry time our bod-ies

meet, com-plete. Long lost feel-ings_____ stir in-side me,_____ used to

think nights were for sleep-ing,_____ Be-ing want-ed_____ is a thrill I nev-er

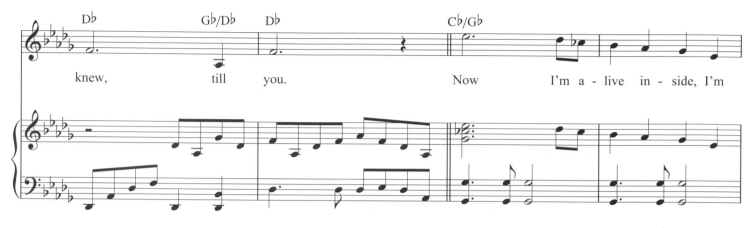

knew, till you. Now I'm a- live in- side, I'm

glow- ing, I'm how I want to be, lov- ing you I can be

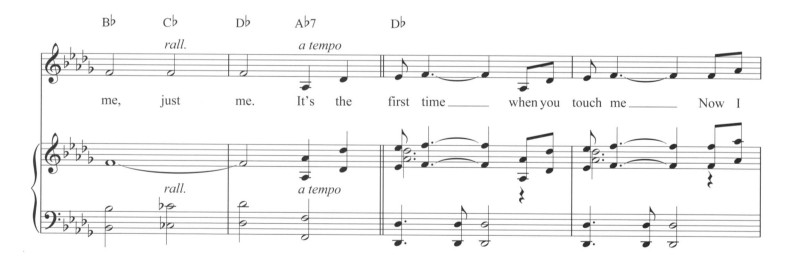

me, just me. It's the first time_____ when you touch me_____ Now I

long for rain- y morn- ings,_____ in each- oth- er_____ we find all we're look- ing for,_____

and more. Found the rain - bow _____ I was af - ter, _____ no more

dreams with one face miss - sing, _____ I am cer - tain _____ you're the last man in my

life _____ I am

cer - tain _____ you're the last man in my life _____

This page has been left blank to facilitate page turns.

THE LAST MAN IN MY LIFE

from *Tell Me on a Sunday*

excerpt

Music by ANDREW LLOYD WEBBER
Lyrics by DON BLACK

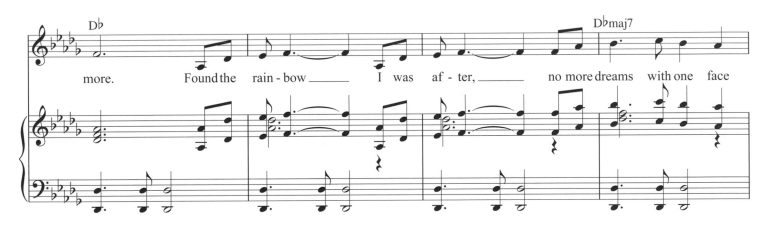

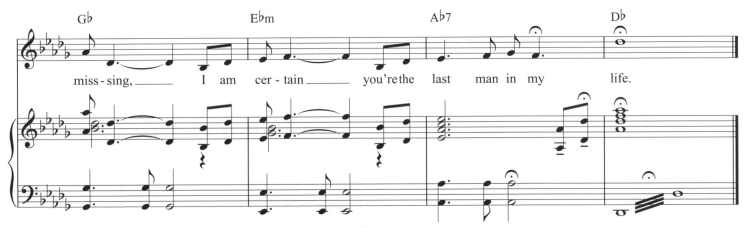

MEMORY
from *Cats*

Music by ANDREW LLOYD WEBBER
Text by TREVOR NUNN after T.S. ELIOT

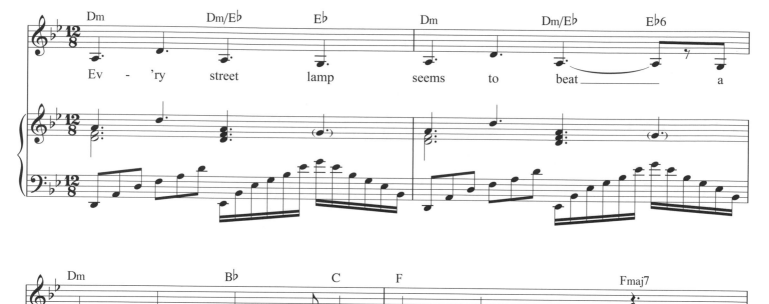

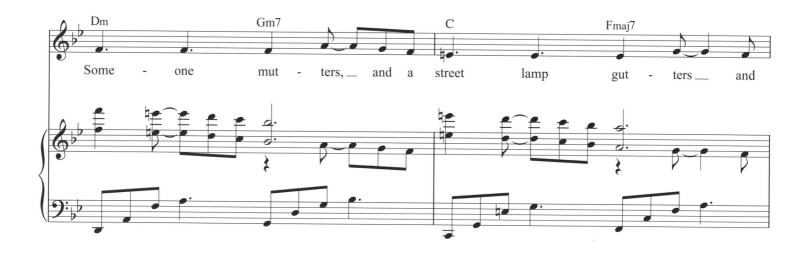

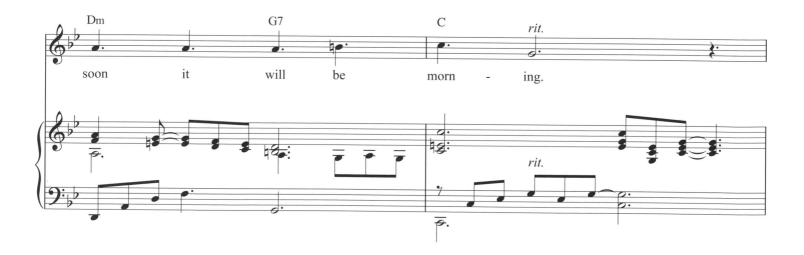

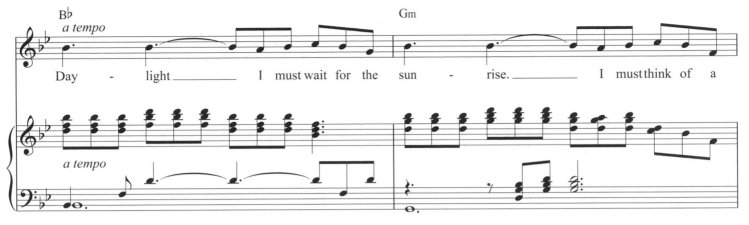

Day - light _____ I must wait for the sun - rise. _____ I must think of a

new life, _____ and I must-n't give in. _____ When the dawn comes to-night will be a

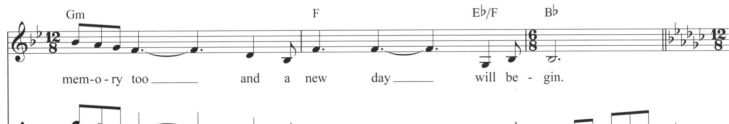

mem-o - ry too _____ and a new day _____ will be - gin.

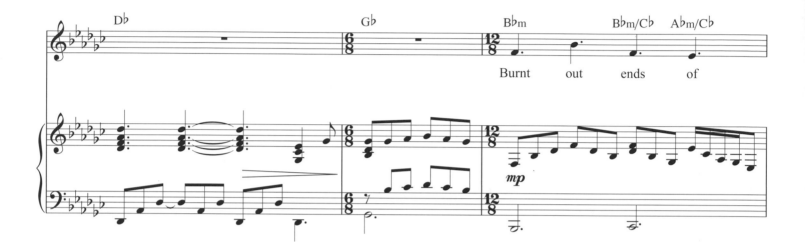

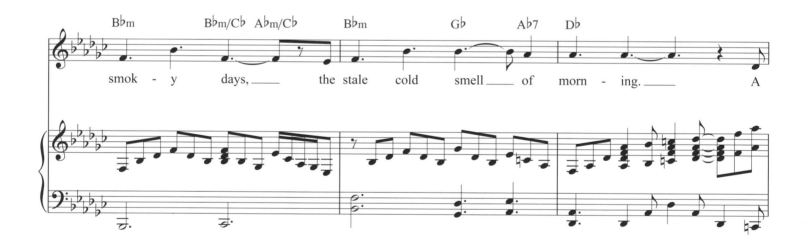

MEMORY
from *Cats*
excerpt

Music by ANDREW LLOYD WEBBER
Text by TREVOR NUNN after T.S. ELIOT

TELL ME ON A SUNDAY

from *Tell Me on a Sunday*

Music by ANDREW LLOYD WEBBER
Lyrics by DON BLACK

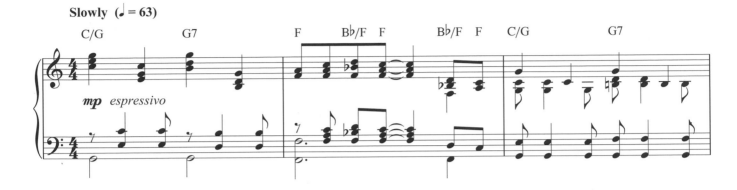

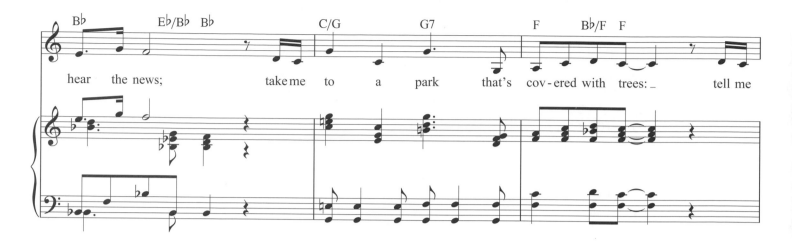

hear the news; take me to a park that's cov-ered with trees: ___ tell me

on a Sun - day please. Let me down eas - y,

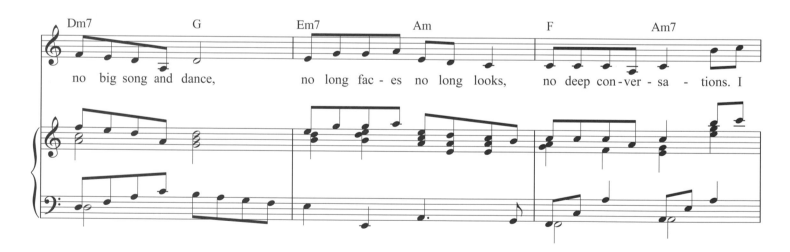

no big song and dance, no long fac - es no long looks, no deep con-ver-sa - tions. I

know the way we should spend the day; take me to a zoo that's

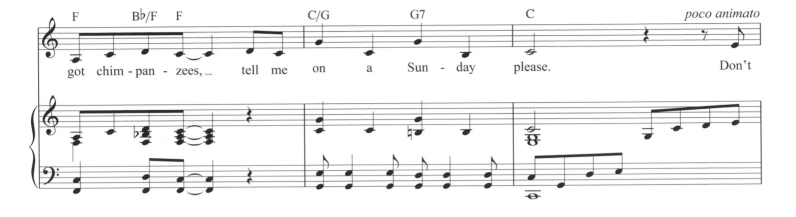

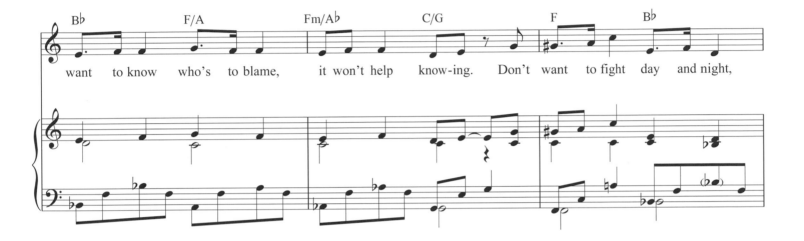

say good-bye. Find a cir - cus ring with a fly-ing tra-peze.＿ Tell me

on a Sun - day please.

I don't want to fight day and night, bad e-nough you're go - ing.

Don't leave in si - lence with no words at all.

Don't get drunk and slam the door, that's no way to end this. I

know how I want you to say good-bye. Don't run off in the pour-ing rain. Don't call

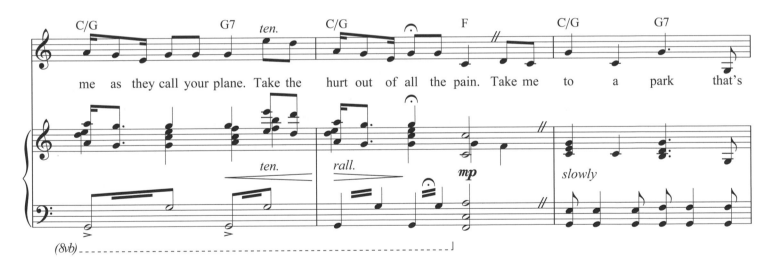

me as they call your plane. Take the hurt out of all the pain. Take me to a park that's

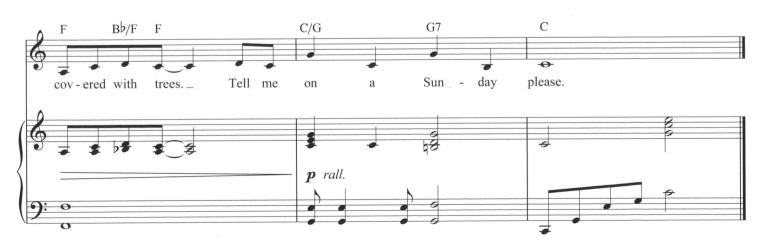

cov-ered with trees.__ Tell me on a Sun-day please.

TELL ME ON A SUNDAY

from *Tell Me on a Sunday*

excerpt

Music by ANDREW LLOYD WEBBER
Lyrics by DON BLACK

say good-bye. Don't run off in the pour-ing rain. Don't call

me as they call your plane. Take the hurt out of all the pain. Take me

Slowly

to a park that's cov-ered with trees.___ Tell me

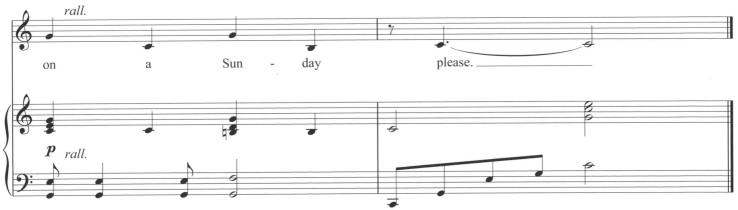

on a Sun-day please.___

Optional ending here to keep closer to 30 seconds.

THINK OF ME
from *The Phantom of the Opera*

Music by ANDREW LLOYD WEBBER
Lyrics by CHARLES HART
Additional Lyrics by RICHARD STILGOE

try.   On that day,_____ that not so dis-tant day,_____ when you are

far a - way and free,   if you ev-er find   a

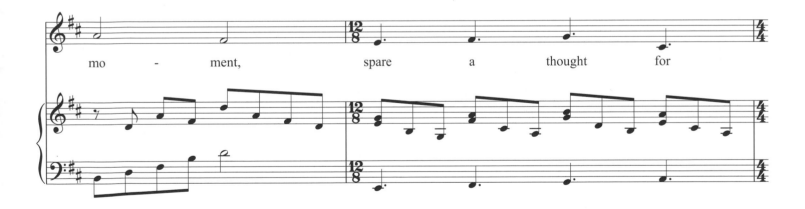

mo -   ment,   spare   a   thought   for

me.

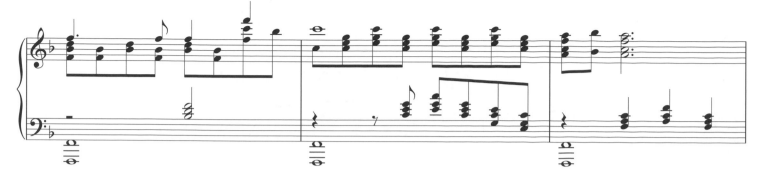

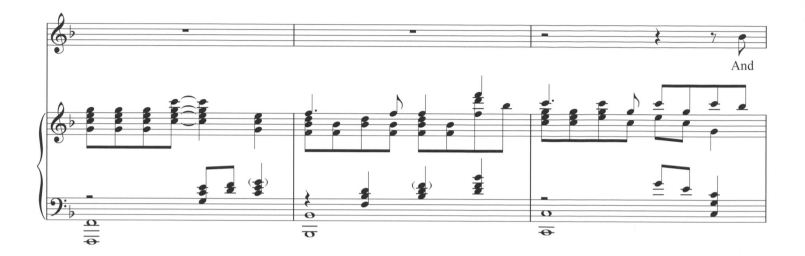

though it's clear, though it was al - ways clear____ that this was nev - er meant to

mp

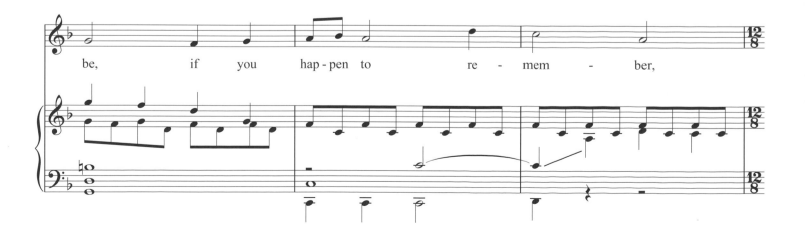

be, if you hap - pen to re - mem - ber,

stop and think of me. Think of

Au - gust when the trees were green; don't

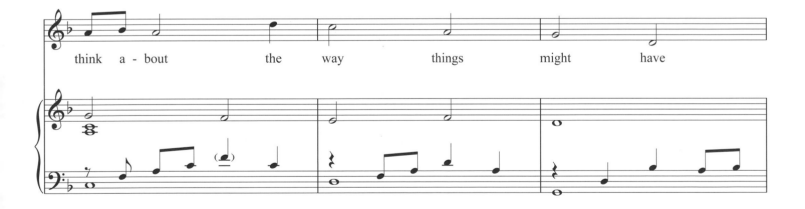

think a - bout the way things might have

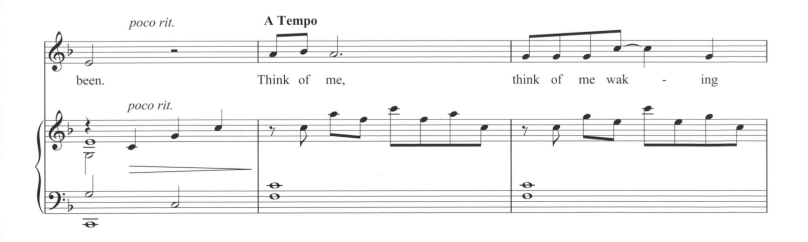

been. Think of me, think of me wak - ing

si - lent and re - signed. I - mag-ine me,

try - ing too hard __ to put you from my mind.

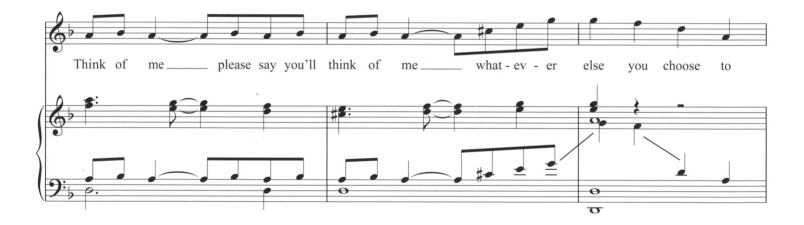

Think of me __ please say you'll think of me __ what - ev - er else you choose to

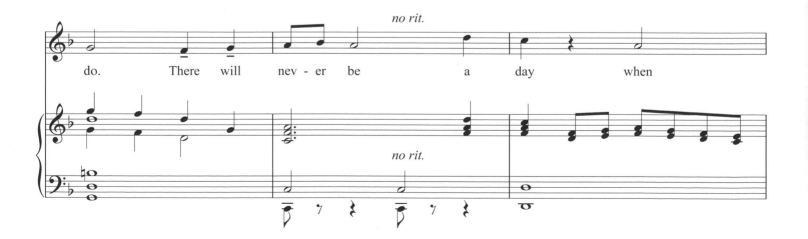

do. There will nev - er be a day when

no rit.

I won't think of you.

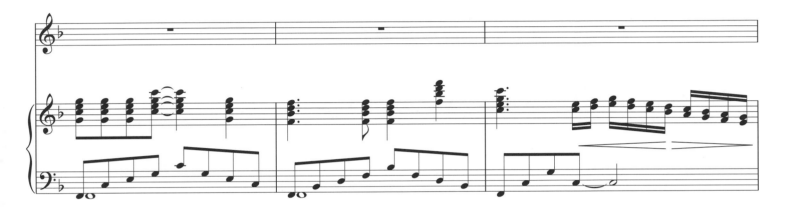

Flow-ers fade,_____ the fruits of sum-mer fade,_____ they have their

sea - son so do we... but please prom - ise me that

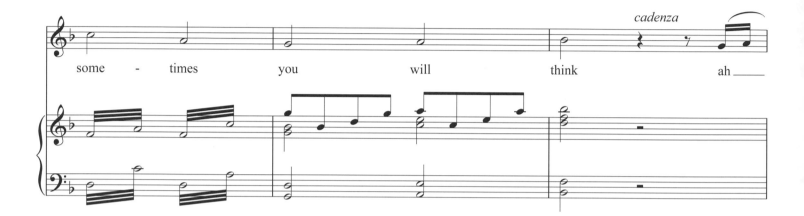

some - times you will think ah ____

ah ____ ah ____

of me!

THINK OF ME
from *The Phantom of the Opera*
excerpt

Music by ANDREW LLOYD WEBBER
Lyrics by CHARLES HART
Additional Lyrics by RICHARD STILGOE

TOO MUCH IN LOVE TO CARE

from *Sunset Boulevard*

Music by ANDREW LLOYD WEBBER
Lyrics by DON BLACK and CHRISTOPHER HAMPTON

This duet for Betty and Joe has been adapted as a solo.

more. If this is real, how should I feel?

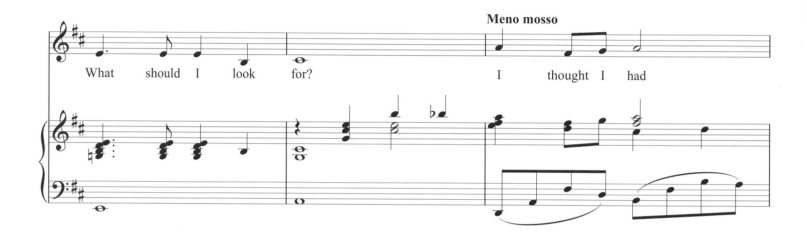

What should I look for? I thought I had

Meno mosso

ev - 'ry-thing I need-ed. My life was set, my dreams were in place.

My heart could see way in - to the fu - ture. All of that goes when

Poco meno mosso

I thought I had ev-'ry-thing I need-ed. My life was set, my

dreams were in place. My heart could see way in-to the fu-ture.

All of that goes when I see your face. This is cra-zy.

You know we should call it a day. Sound ad-vice, great ad-vice, let's throw it a-way.

I can't con-trol all the things I'm feel-ing. We're float-ing in mid -

air. If we are fools, well, we're too much in love to

care. If we are fools, well, we're too much in

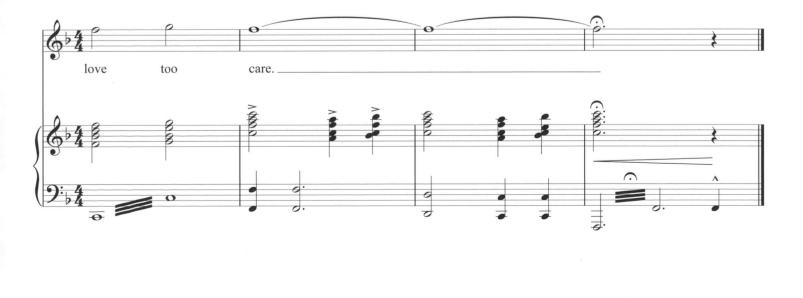

love too care.

This page has been left blank to facilitate page turns.

TOO MUCH IN LOVE TO CARE

from *Sunset Boulevard*

excerpt

Music by ANDREW LLOYD WEBBER
Lyrics by DON BLACK and CHRISTOPHER HAMPTON

UNEXPECTED SONG
from *Song & Dance*

Music by ANDREW LLOYD WEBBER
Lyrics by DON BLACK

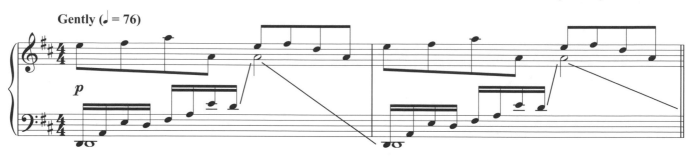

I have nev-er felt like this, for once I'm lost for
I don't know what's go-ing on, can't work it out at

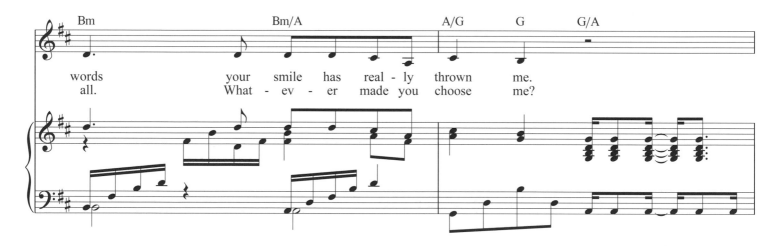

words. your smile has real-ly thrown me.
all. What-ev-er made you choose me?

This is not like me at all, I nev-er thought I'd
I just can't be-lieve my eyes, you look at me as

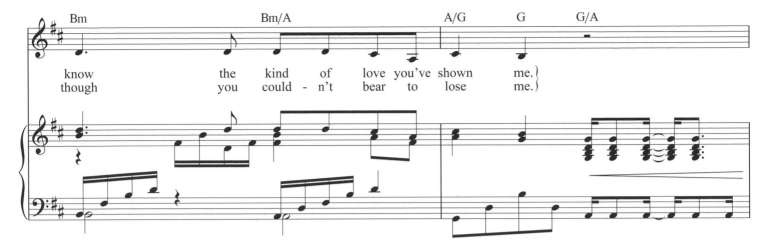

know the kind of love you've shown me.
though you could -n't bear to lose me.

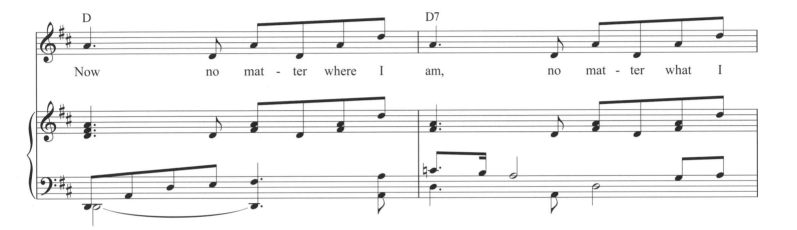

Now no mat -ter where I am, no mat -ter what I

do, I see your face ap -pear -ing

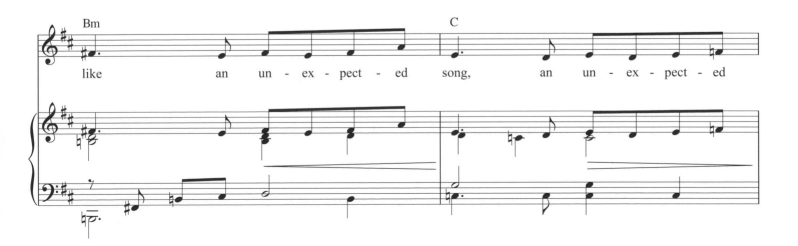

like an un -ex -pect -ed song, an un -ex -pect -ed

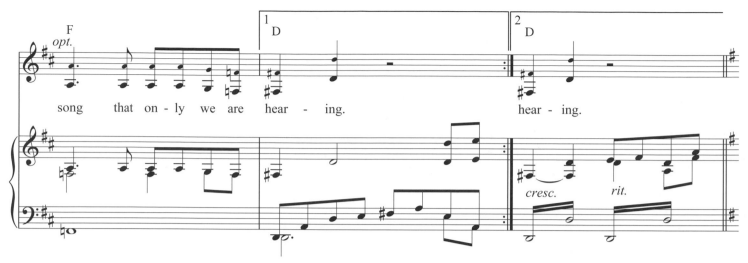

song that on - ly we are hear - ing.   hear - ing.

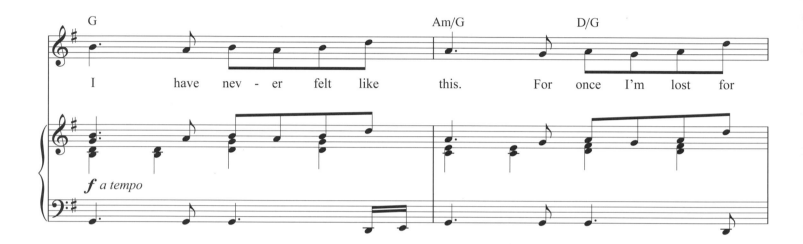

I have nev - er felt like this. For once I'm lost for

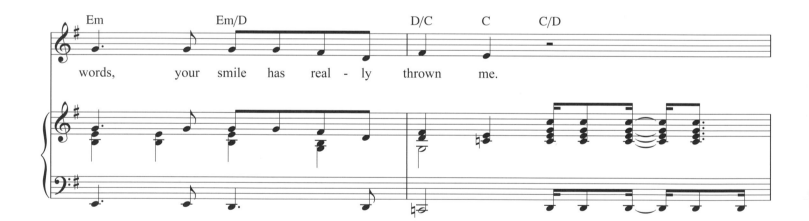

words, your smile has real - ly thrown me.

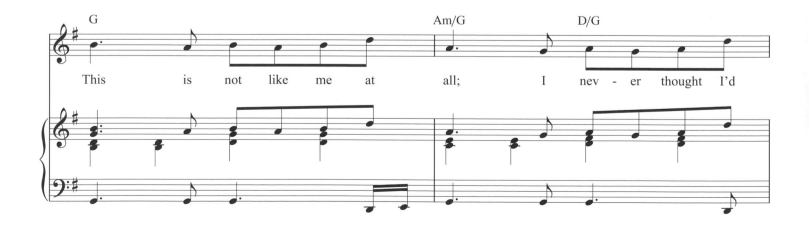

This is not like me at all; I nev - er thought I'd

know the kind of love you've shown me.

Now no mat - ter where I am, no mat - ter what I

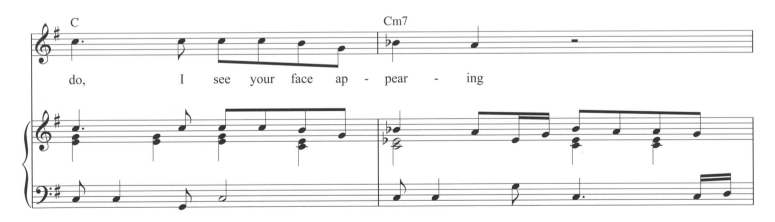

do, I see your face ap - pear - ing

like an un - ex - pect - ed song, an un - ex - pect - ed

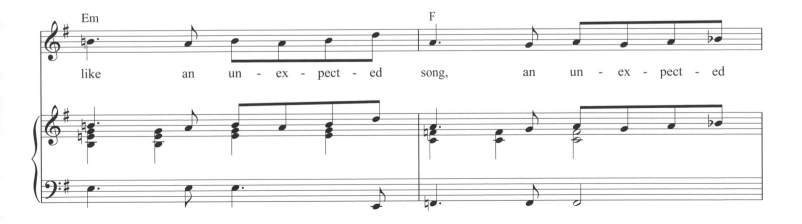

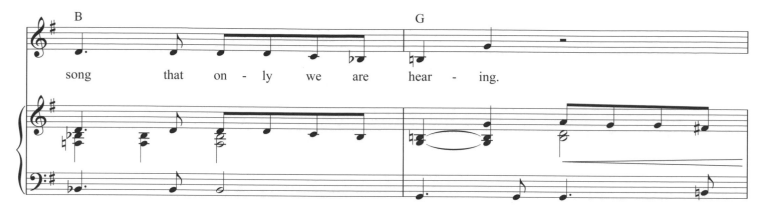

song that on - ly we are hear - ing.

Like an un - ex - pect - ed song, an un - ex - pect - ed

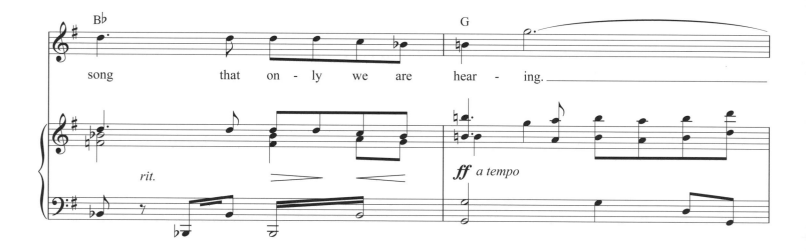

song that on - ly we are hear - ing.

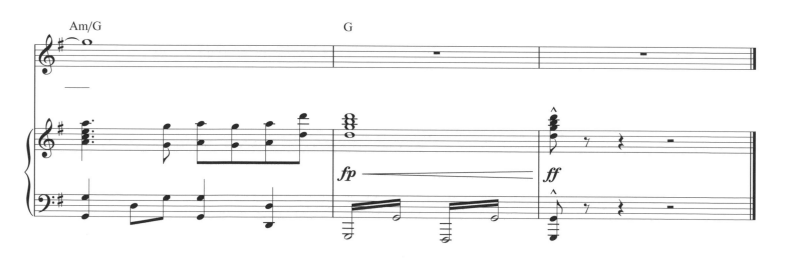

UNEXPECTED SONG
from *Song & Dance*
excerpt

Music by ANDREW LLOYD WEBBER
Lyrics by DON BLACK

Gently ♩ = 76

EMMA:

Now no mat-ter where I am, no mat-ter what I
do, I see your face ap-pear-ing like an un-ex-pect-ed song, an un-ex-pect-ed

song that on-ly we are hear-ing. Like an un-ex-pect-ed

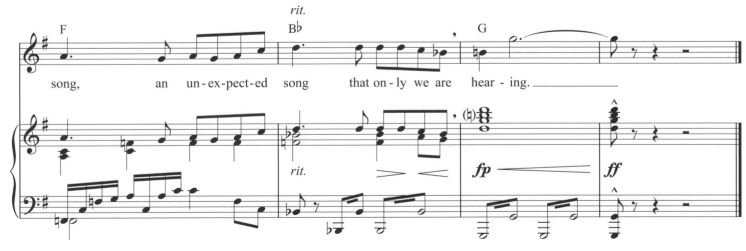

song, an un-ex-pect-ed song that on-ly we are hear-ing.

WISHING YOU WERE SOMEHOW HERE AGAIN

from *The Phantom of the Opera*

Music by ANDREW LLOYD WEBBER
Lyrics by CHARLES HART
Additional Lyrics by RICHARD STILGOE

if I just dreamed, some-how you would be here.

Wish-ing I could hear your voice a-gain, know-ing that I nev - er

would, dream-ing of you won't help me to do all that you dreamed I

could. Pass - ing bells and sculpt - ed an-gels, cold and mon - u -

men - tal, seem for you the wrong com-pan-ions; you were warm and

rit.

gen - tle.

a tempo

pp *a tempo*

Too man - y years fight-ing back tears, why can't the past just

die?

Wish-ing you were some - how here a - gain,

ff

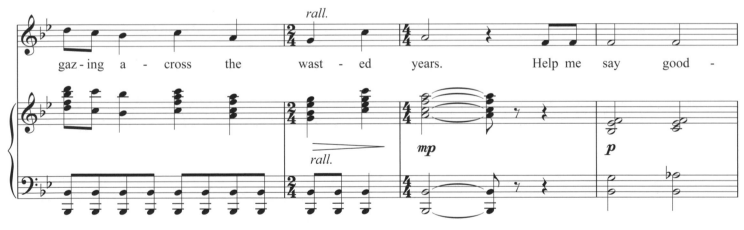

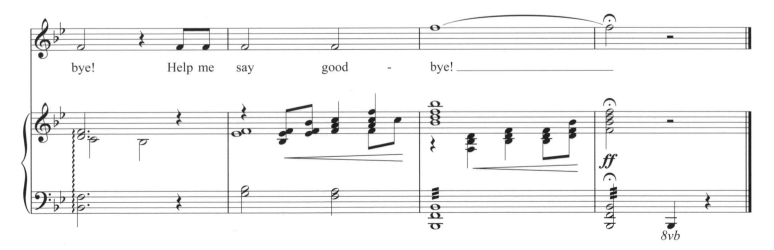

WISHING YOU WERE SOMEHOW HERE AGAIN

from *The Phantom of the Opera*

excerpt

Music by ANDREW LLOYD WEBBER
Lyrics by CHARLES HART
Additional Lyrics by RICHARD STILGOE

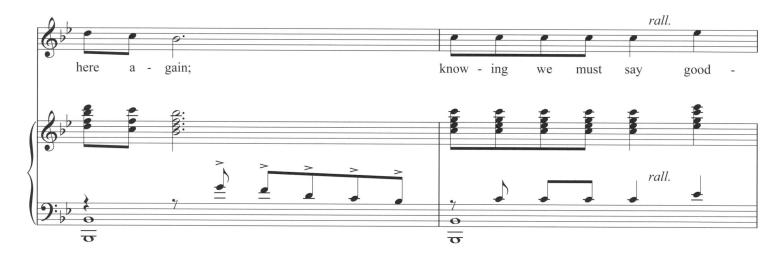

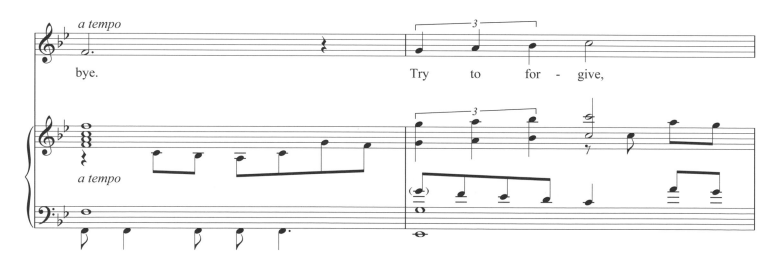

teach me to live, give me the strength to try. No more

mem-o-ries no more si-lent tears, no more gaz-ing a-cross the

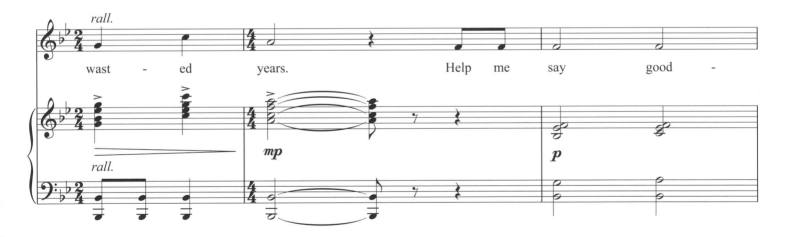

wast - ed years. Help me say good -

bye! Help me say good - bye!

WITH ONE LOOK
from *Sunset Boulevard*

Music by ANDREW LLOYD WEBBER
Lyrics by DON BLACK and CHRISTOPHER HAMPTON,
with contributions by AMY POWERS

or the love that you've hun - gered for. When I speak it's with my

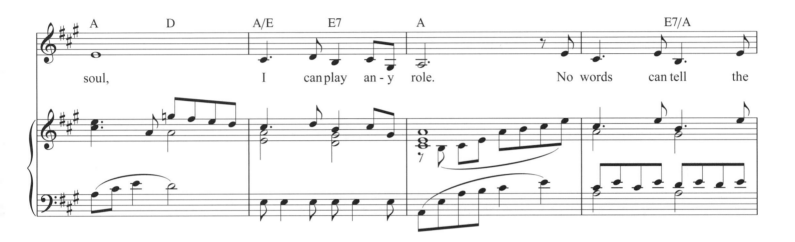

soul, I can play an - y role. No words can tell the

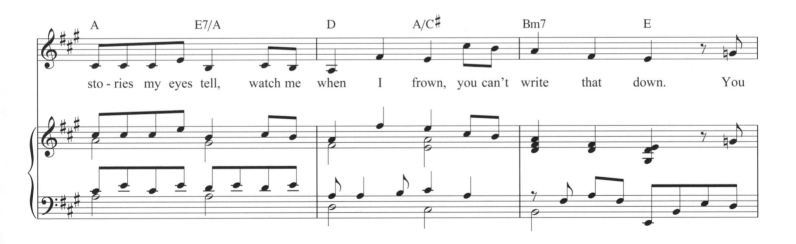

sto - ries my eyes tell, watch me when I frown, you can't write that down. You

know I'm right, it's there in black and white, when I look your way you'll hear

what I say. Yes, with one look I put words to shame,

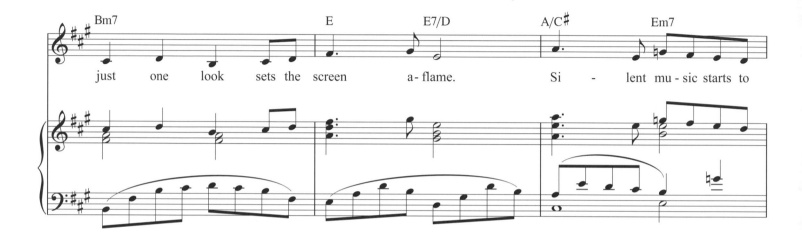

just one look sets the screen a-flame. Si - lent mu - sic starts to

play, one tear in my eye makes the whole world cry.

With one look they'll for - give the past, they'll re - joice I've re -

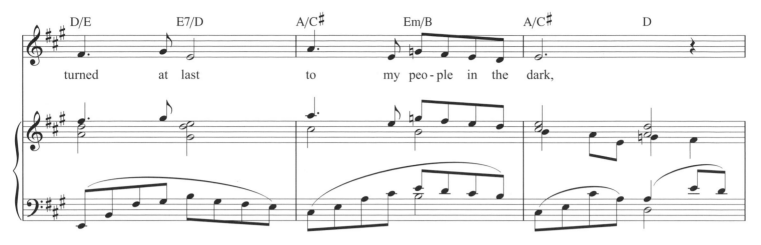

turned at last to my peo - ple in the dark,

still out there in the dark.

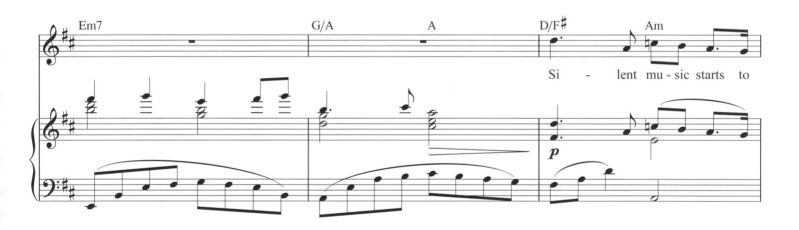

Si - lent mu - sic starts to

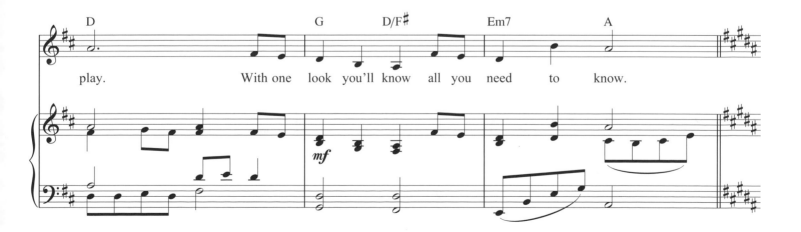

play. With one look you'll know all you need to know.

With one look I'll ig-nite a blaze, I'll re-turn to my

glo-ry days. They'll say Nor-ma's back at last.

This time I am stay-ing, I'm stay-ing for good, I'll be back where I was born to

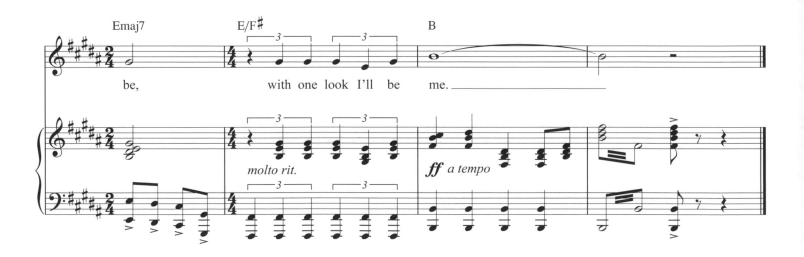

be, with one look I'll be me.

WITH ONE LOOK

from *Sunset Boulevard*

excerpt

Music by ANDREW LLOYD WEBBER
Lyrics by DON BLACK and CHRISTOPHER HAMPTON,
with contributions by AMY POWERS

YOU MUST LOVE ME
from the Cinergi Motion Picture *Evita*

Words by TIM RICE
Music by ANDREW LLOYD WEBBER

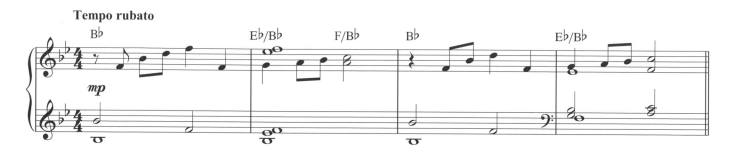

pear. What do we do___ for our dream to sur- vive?

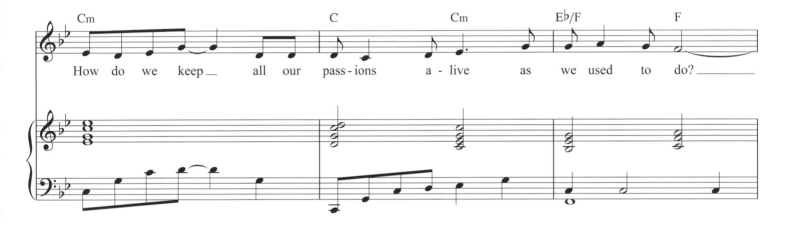

How do we keep___ all our pass - ions a - live as we used to do?_____

Deep in my heart I'm con - ceal - ing things that I'm long-ing to

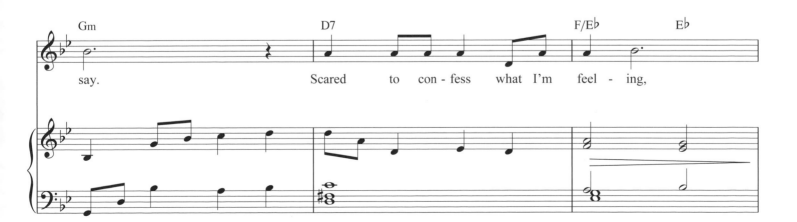

say. Scared to con - fess what I'm feel - ing,

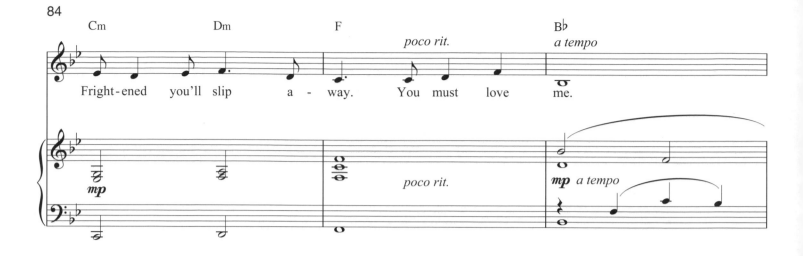

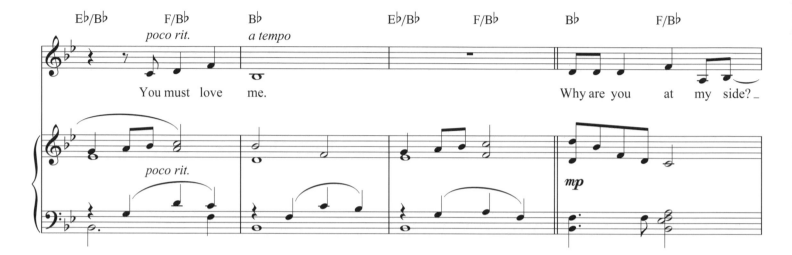

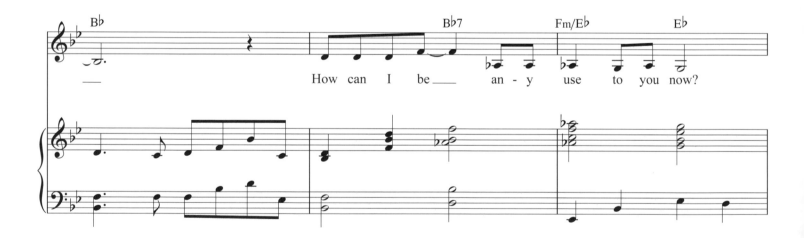

Deep in my heart I'm con-ceal - ing

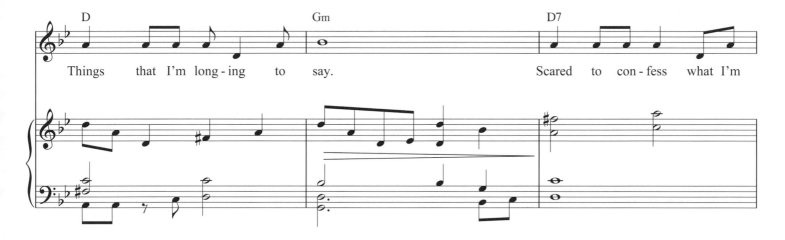

Things that I'm long-ing to say. Scared to con-fess what I'm

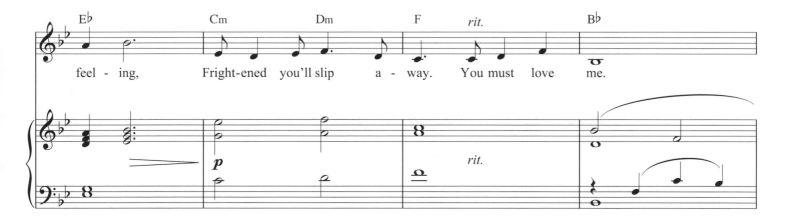

feel-ing, Fright-ened you'll slip a - way. You must love me.

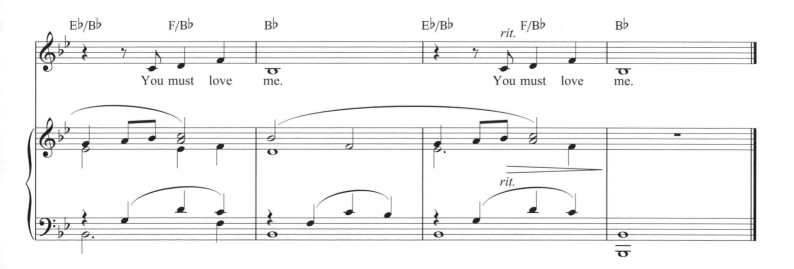

You must love me. You must love me.

YOU MUST LOVE ME
from the Cinergi Motion Picture *Evita*
excerpt

Words by TIM RICE
Music by ANDREW LLOYD WEBBER

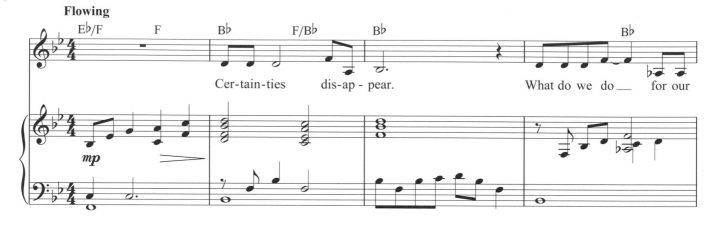